GW00888624

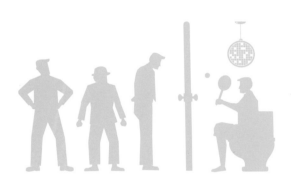

HOW TO

AVOID
BOREDOM
ON THE LOO

WHILE YOU MAKE
NASTY SMELLS

igloobooks

igloobooks

Published in 2020
by Igloo Books Ltd
Cottage Farm
Sywell
NN6 0BJ
www.igloobooks.com

0920 001
2 4 6 8 10 9 7 5 3 1
ISBN 978-1-83903-421-3

Cover, title pages, p3, 145 and 146 imagery: © iStock / Getty Images
All other interior images courtesy of Shutterstock

Designed by Simon Parker
Edited by Claire Ormsby-Potter

Printed and manufactured in China

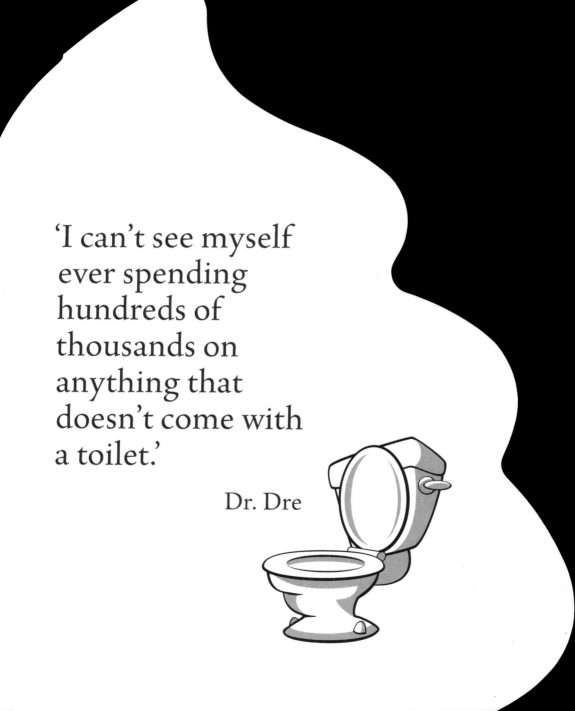

'I can't see myself ever spending hundreds of thousands on anything that doesn't come with a toilet.'

Dr. Dre

Are you sitting comfortably?

thunderbox

bog ladies' gents'

A loo by any other name
would smell as sweet

water closet or WC little boys' room

throne room restroom smallest room

outhouse garderobe honey bucket

lavatory (posh)

toilet (not posh)

sh*tter (really not posh)

powder room | convenience

little girls' room | cloakroom | bathroom

dunny | pissoir (French) | latrine | can

head | ablutions

John | brasco | bogger | lav

crapper | privy | cloakroom | washroom

The oldest known functioning loo is around 4,000 years old. You can see it in the Minoan Palace of Knossos, Crete. (But you can't use it!)

In a public convenience, which loo is the cleanest?

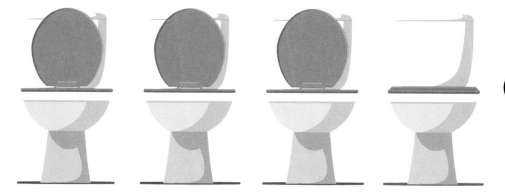

The Power of 3

The average person spends three years of their life on the loo.

Pooing between three times a day and three times a week is considered normal.

A third of people flush while still sitting on the loo.

A human expels
3 lb of poo a day.
Compare that to an
elephant's 300 lb.

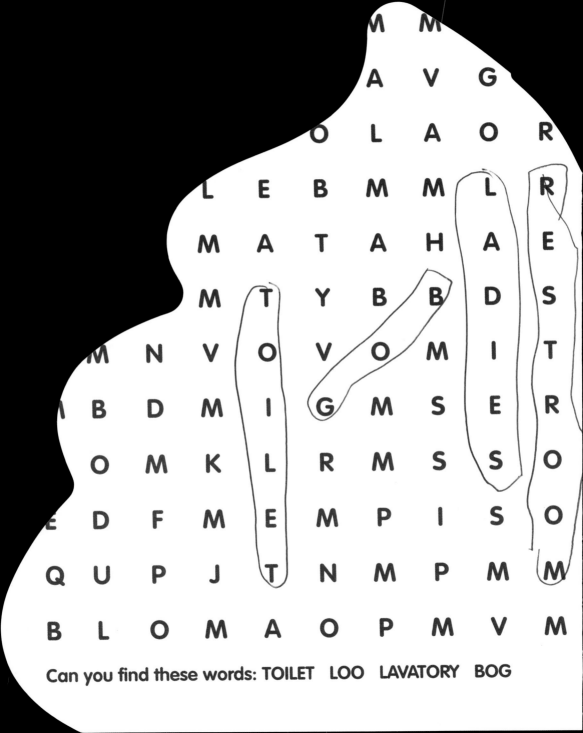

		M	M			
		A	V	G		
	O	L	A	O	R	
L	E	B	M	M	L	R
M	A	T	A	H	A	E
M	T	Y	B	B	D	S
M N V O V O M I T
B D M I G M S E R
O M K L R M S S O
E D F M E M P I S O
Q U P J T N M P M M
B L O M A O P M V M

Can you find these words: TOILET LOO LAVATORY BOG

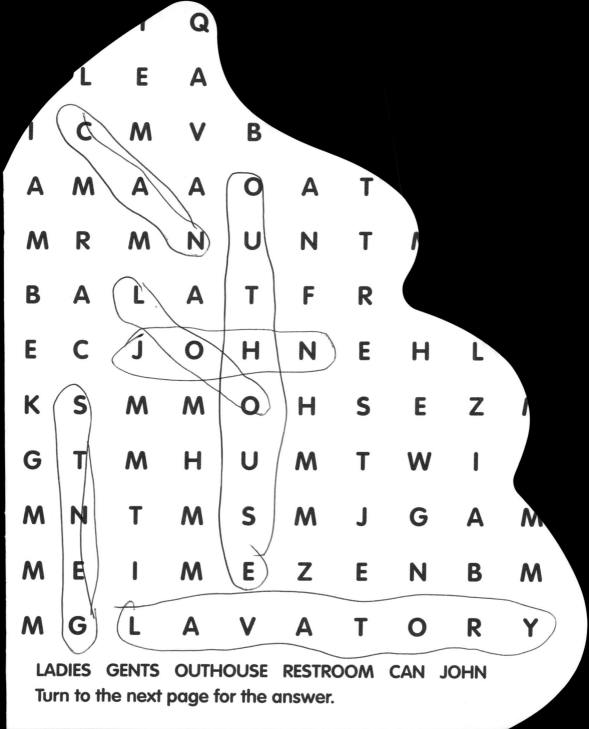

LADIES GENTS OUTHOUSE RESTROOM CAN JOHN

Turn to the next page for the answer.

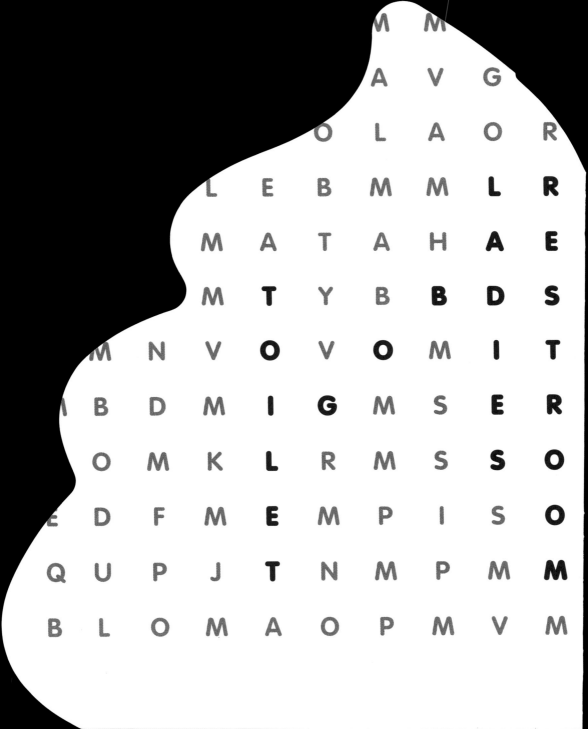

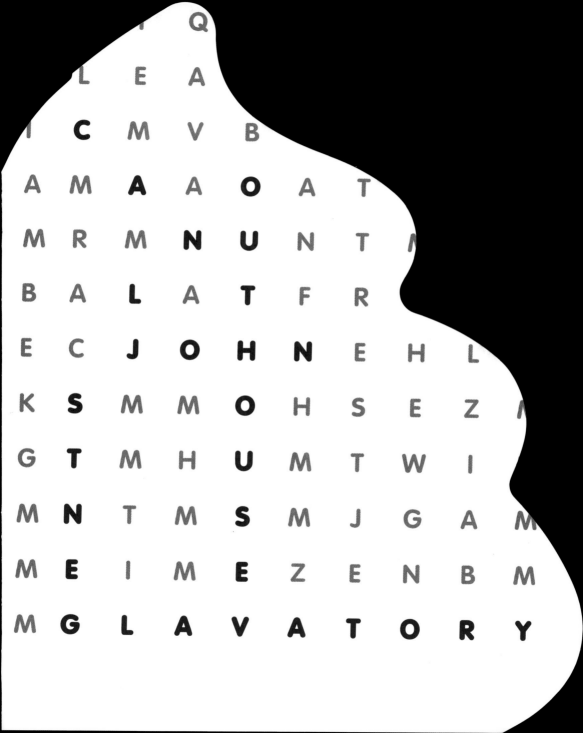

In 2016, the Italian sculptor Maurizio Cattelan created a work he named *America*: an 18-carat solid gold toilet that he encouraged art fans to use when they visited the gallery.

It hit the headlines in 2019 when it was stolen from an art exhibition at Blenheim Palace.

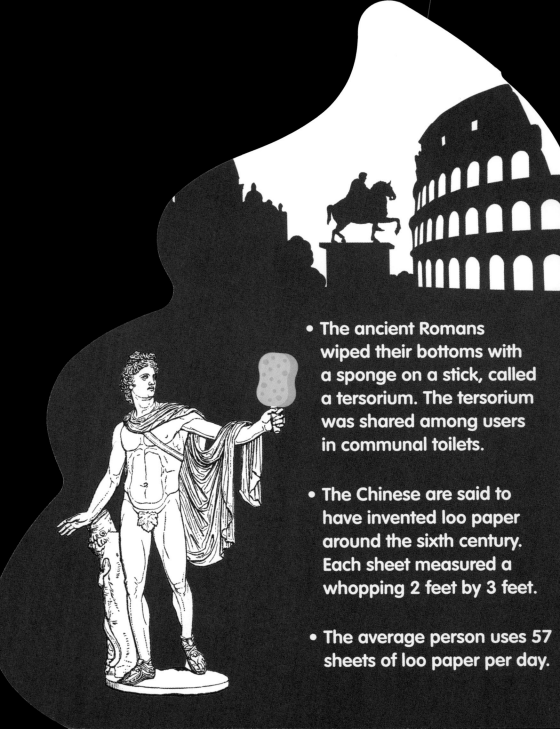

- The ancient Romans wiped their bottoms with a sponge on a stick, called a tersorium. The tersorium was shared among users in communal toilets.

- The Chinese are said to have invented loo paper around the sixth century. Each sheet measured a whopping 2 feet by 3 feet.

- The average person uses 57 sheets of loo paper per day.

- **The first toilet paper to be developed and sold in England appeared in 1880. It was sold as individual sheets in a box, like a box of tissues today.**

- **Loo paper on a roll was first manufactured around 1890 by the Scott Paper Company.**

The average person goes
to the loo six to eight times
a day, or approximately
2,500 times a year.

Poo jokes aren't
my favourite,
but they are
a solid number **2**.

ROYAL FLUSH

The ancient Egyptians thought poo had magical powers. A trusted servant had the job of burying the pharaoh's poo safely to stop it falling into the hands of magicians who could use it to harm him.

'My wife and I were married in a toilet – it was a marriage of convenience!'

Tommy Cooper

Do you know your poo?

The shape of your poo is dependent on how long it remains in your colon. Unofficially, there are seven types of number 2.

Where do you fit?

Type 1 & 2

1. Separate hard lumps that look a bit like nuts.

2. A sausage shape that's lumpy.

These are signs of constipation.

Type 3 & 4

3. A sausage with cracks on its surface.

4. The holy grail: a smooth, slightly softer sausage.

You're perfectly normal.

Type 5

5. Soft blobs of poo with defined edges.

You're beyond normal but don't have diarrhoea.

Type 6 & 7

6. Fluffy pieces with ragged edges that verge on the mushy.

7. Watery liquid with no solid pieces – full-blown diarrhoea.

Oh dear, you'd better not go too far away from the loo!

What's in your pee?

Pee is around 95 per cent water, but it contains a staggering 3,079 compounds. Of those, 72 come from bacteria and a further 1,453 from your body. Another 2,282 come from our diet, drugs, cosmetics and the environment.

Who knew?

Why is there no toilet paper at KFC?

Because it's finger lickin' good!

Which is the most hygienic way to dry your hands?

a. Drying them with paper towels.

b. Drying them with a hand towel.

c. Drying them with an air dryer.

When you gotta go, you gotta go...

These famous people died on (or near) the loo:

Elvis Presley, Lenny Bruce,
Judy Garland, Evelyn Waugh,
George II of Great Britain, Louis Khan,
Don Simpson, Lupe Velez
and Catherine the Great.

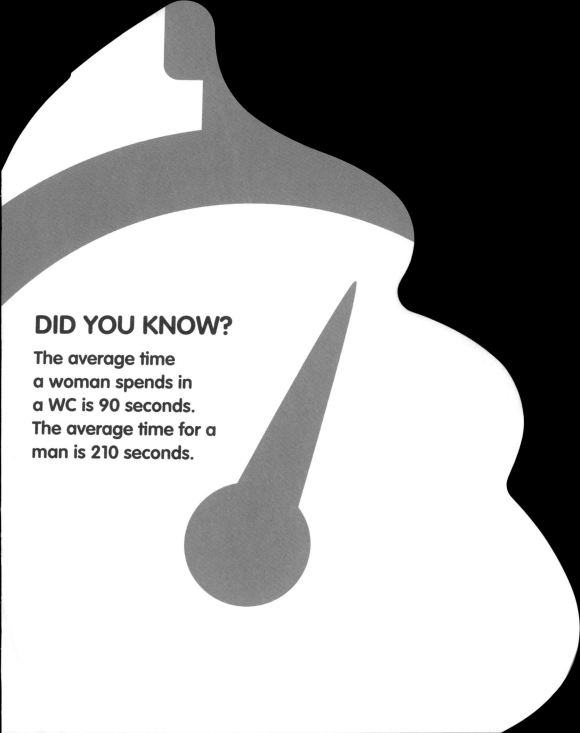

DID YOU KNOW?

The average time
a woman spends in
a WC is 90 seconds.
The average time for a
man is 210 seconds.

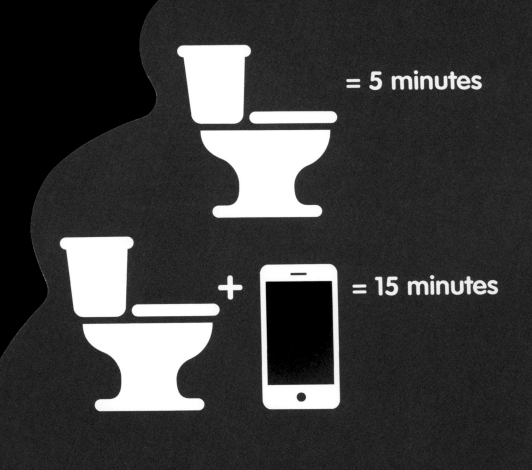

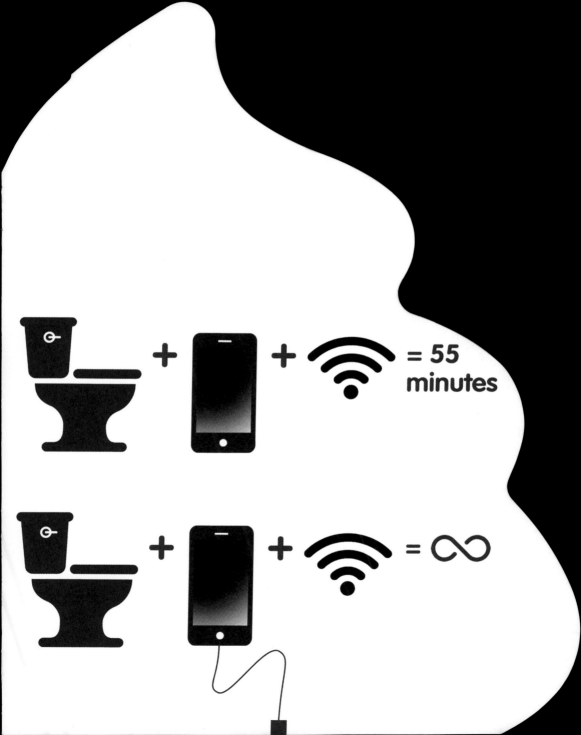

**What did one fly
say to another one?**

Is that stool taken?

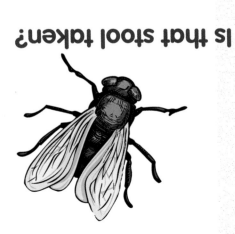

MOVIE MOMENT

One of the grossest scenes in movie history comes in *Trainspotting*. Drug-addict Renton, played by Ewan McGregor, is caught short when his constipation comes to a sudden end and takes a swim inside a filthy, faeces-caked loo.

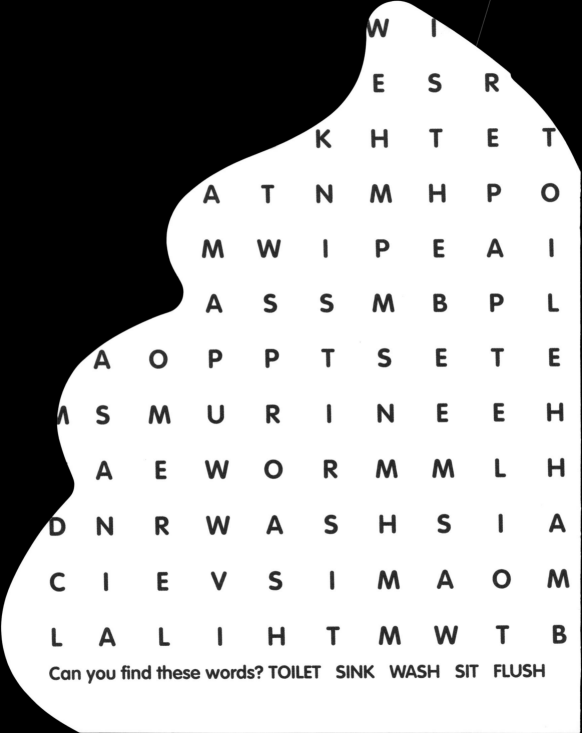

Can you find these words? TOILET   SINK   WASH   SIT   FLUSH

```
        H   M
    M   A   L
M   M   N   P   M   
M   M   G   O   H   S   T
M   M   T   M   M   M   T
F   L   U   S   H   G   A
O   K   H   M   M   R   Y   Y   E
S   O   A   P   M   A   R   N   D
L   N   B   I   M   M   D   A   I
M   T   B   I   D   E   T   M   B   M
R   O   M   P   E   L   O   T   M   N
M   M   M   T   E   L   I   O   T   I
```

DRY SOAP WIPE TOILET PAPER BIDET URINE

Turn to the next page for the answer.

H	M
M	A	L
M	M	N	P	M
M	M	G	O	H	S	T
M	M	T	M	M	M	T	T
F	L	U	S	H	G	A
O	K	H	M	M	R	Y	Y	E
S	O	A	P	M	A	R	N	D
L	N	B	I	M	M	D	A	I
M	T	B	I	D	E	T	M	B	M
R	O	M	P	E	L	O	T	M	N
M	M	M	T	E	L	I	O	T	I

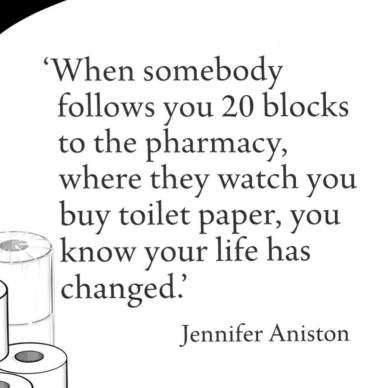

'When somebody follows you 20 blocks to the pharmacy, where they watch you buy toilet paper, you know your life has changed.'

Jennifer Aniston

The Spanish village of
El Vendrell installed a
public toilet solely for
dogs to make it
quicker and
easier to
clean up
after them.

Did you hear about the new movie *Constipation*?

No one knows if it will ever come out.

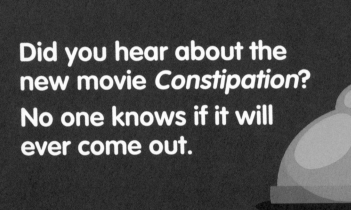

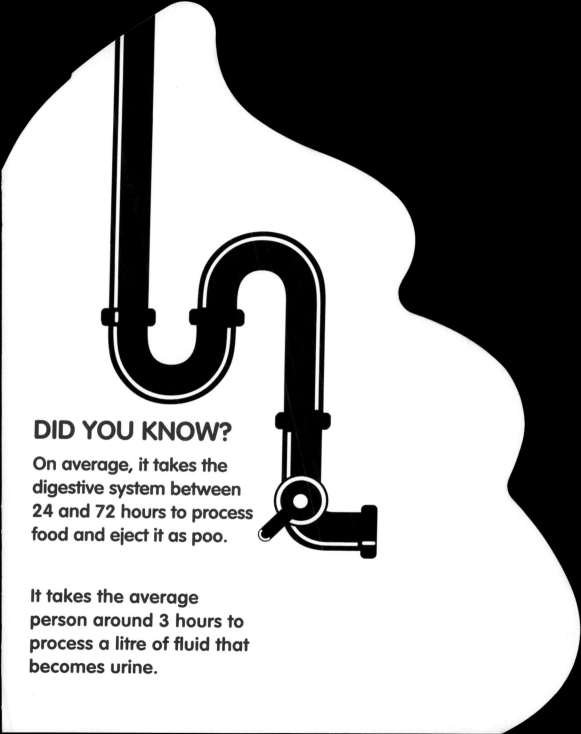

DID YOU KNOW?

On average, it takes the digestive system between 24 and 72 hours to process food and eject it as poo.

It takes the average person around 3 hours to process a litre of fluid that becomes urine.

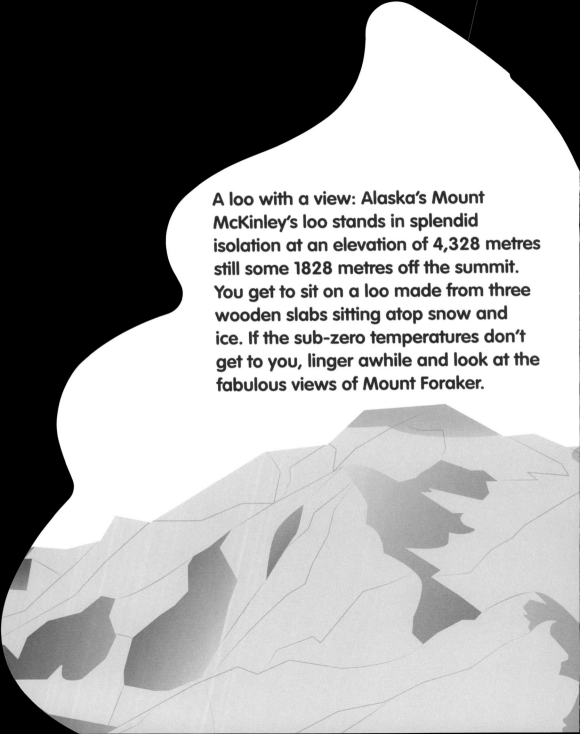

A loo with a view: Alaska's Mount McKinley's loo stands in splendid isolation at an elevation of 4,328 metres still some 1828 metres off the summit. You get to sit on a loo made from three wooden slabs sitting atop snow and ice. If the sub-zero temperatures don't get to you, linger awhile and look at the fabulous views of Mount Foraker.

ROYAL FLUSH

Diana, Princess of Wales, made it a rule of royal duty to always use the loo when she saw one. She reasoned that there was no telling when there might be another chance!

If you ever feel powerless, just remember that a single one of your pubic hairs can shut down an entire restaurant.

'The toilets at a local police station have been stolen. Police say they have nothing to go on.'

Ronnie Barker

HISTORY

All loos were unisex until 1739, when at a posh party in Paris there were separate facilities for girls and boys for the first time.

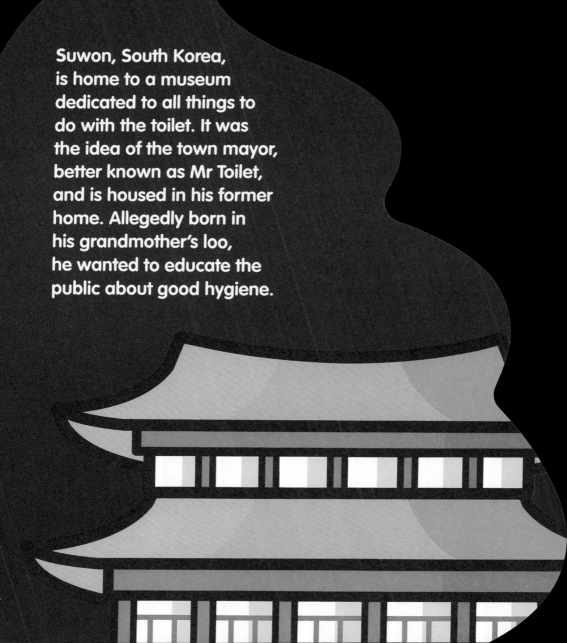

Suwon, South Korea, is home to a museum dedicated to all things to do with the toilet. It was the idea of the town mayor, better known as Mr Toilet, and is housed in his former home. Allegedly born in his grandmother's loo, he wanted to educate the public about good hygiene.

Sanitation

Which has the least bacteria on it at any time?

a. mobile phone

b. loo seat

c. tv remote control

d. kitchen chopping board

The answer is B. loo seat. A chopping board has 200 per cent more poo bacteria than a loo seat. Mobiles have, on average, ten times more bacteria than loo seats and remotes generally have more bacteria than private loos.

The sixth-century BC Chinese ruler Duke Jing of Jin was warned by a soothsayer that he could come to a premature end. Disturbed by the nightmares this caused, the duke began to wander the palace at night – which is how he fell into the slurry pit beneath the WC and drowned in excrement.

DID YOU KNOW?

According to official British guidelines, the recommended provision of public lavatories is one cubicle per 10,000 population.

The recommended maximum waiting time in a British public convenience is 2 minutes. Remember to set your timer!

Help Lucy get to the loo before it's too late!

Turn to the next page for the answer.

Did she get there?

The world's most expensive loo was designed for NASA's International Space Station. It has thigh bars and leg restraints to stop astronauts from floating off the seat while they push.

The loo then dries the solid waste to eliminate bacteria and smells and filters the urine into drinking water. You can have your own – for a mere $19 million.

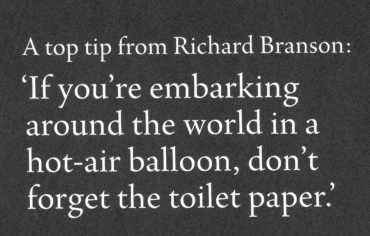

A top tip from Richard Branson:

'If you're embarking around the world in a hot-air balloon, don't forget the toilet paper.'

Did you hear about the
constipated composer?

He had problems with
his last movement.

Can you find these words? PEE URINE WATER URINATION

M M
Y Z N
X Y T Z W D
C R S A E D P
R A F W E X C I
E N P E W L S S
L I M B E A L D S
D R A O E R A D E
D U O H E M S O P
I M C T I M H L L Z
P M A M S I K S Q X
M W E X C E T I O N

WEEWEE   PIDDLE   EXCRETION   WEE   URINARY   SLASH   WAZZ

Turn to the next page for the answer.

```
            M   M
          W   A   Z
        A   Z   Z   Y   O
      E   L   L   I   C   E   I
      R   K   Q   P   E   E   T
      A   M   M   W   N   M   M
  M   W   A   Z   Z   G   I   U   Z
M   M   C   U   O   O   I   R   M   B
    M   R   E   A   M   L   U   H   M
M   U   R   I   N   A   T   I   O   N
    A   W   U   R   I   E   N   M   M   A
    A   E   X   C   R   E   T   I   O   N
```

M M
Y Z N
X Y T Z W D
C R S A E D P
R A F W E X C
E N P E W L S
L I M B E A L D S
D R A O E R A D E M
D U O H E M S O P
I M C T I M H L L Z
P M A M S I K S Q X
M W E X C E T I O N

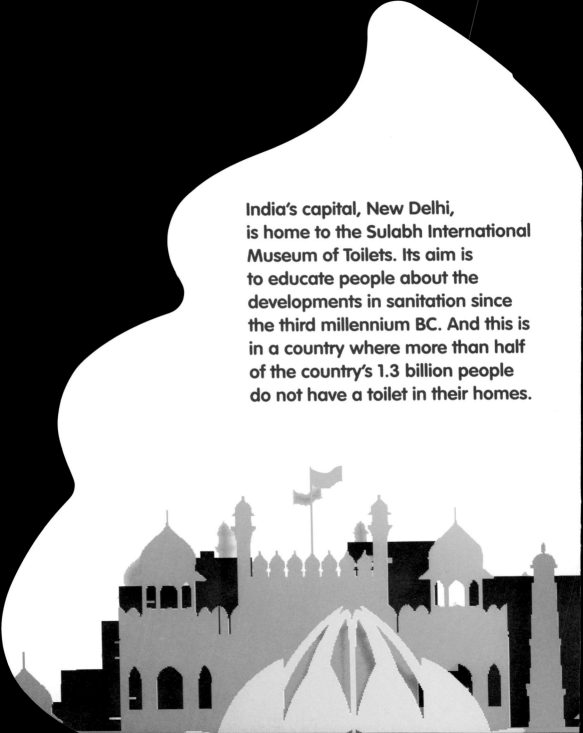

India's capital, New Delhi, is home to the Sulabh International Museum of Toilets. Its aim is to educate people about the developments in sanitation since the third millennium BC. And this is in a country where more than half of the country's 1.3 billion people do not have a toilet in their homes.

In Tudor England, one of the most important court officials was the Groom of the Stool. He was expected to assist the king with all aspects of excretion and ablution. Later, the groom became an important court official.

The Victorians were said to be so prudish they changed the title, so the official was named the Groom of the Stole.

The first air fresheners designed to keep the loo smelling sweet were pomegranates stuffed with cloves.

Today, you can buy a 100ml botanical bathroom deodoriser, or 'post poo drops', for £20. Your visitors will thank you.

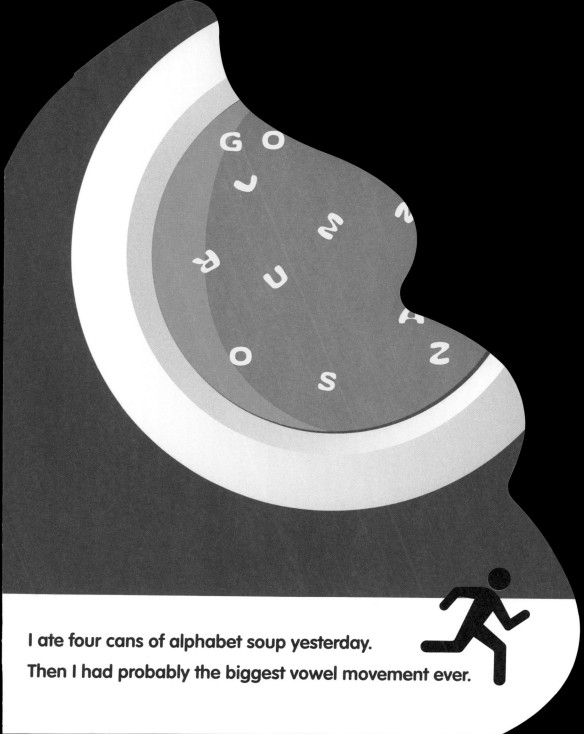

I ate four cans of alphabet soup yesterday.
Then I had probably the biggest vowel movement ever.

The ideal stool colour should be deep chocolate.

Poo smells because it contains sulphur-rich compounds indole, skatole, mercaptans and hydrogen sulfide gas. What you eat affects the smells you make. Sulphur-rich foods, like eggs, meat and milk, can make faeces smell worse.

DID YOU KNOW?

It was only in 1848 that every new house built in England was legally required to have its own loo.

Discovered in Argentina in 2013,
the world's oldest public toilet is some
240 million years old. It is a communal
latrine used by giant rhino-like herbivore
dinosaurs. The discovery proved that
mega-sized reptiles shared their
dumping ground.

Bob is busting for the loo – help him to find his way.

Turn to the next page for the answer.

Did he make it?

Microsoft founder and philanthropist Bill Gates went on TV to promote an ingenious machine that turns human faeces into drinking water. It was all part of Gates' efforts to improve sanitation in undeveloped countries.

Children are like farts.

Your own are just about bearable,
but everyone else's are horrendous.

DID YOU KNOW?

The recommended ratio of stalls to urinals in a male public toilet is 1 to 4.

The average width allowed per user at a trough urinal is 700 mm.

The average time a man stands at a urinal is 35 seconds.

'In politics, you're like a
toilet seat: you're up one
day and down the next.'

Doug Ford

FAMOUS LOOS

The Elizabethan poet Sir John Harington irritated his godmother Elizabeth I with his poor poetry, so he tried to win back her favour by inventing the first flushing lavatory. The water closet had a pan with an opening at the bottom and was flushed with water from a cistern. The queen quite liked it – but the public stuck to chamber pots.

Game of Thrones actor, Kit Harington, who plays Jon Snow, is descended from Sir John Harington, inventor of the first flushing throne! (see previous page)

What do you call
a magical poop?

Poodini

DID YOU KNOW?

On average, 40,000 Americans are injured every day in accidents in the bathroom.

'You know you're big when you sit in the bathtub and the water in the toilet rises.'

Art Donovan

Toilet paper – what a rip off!

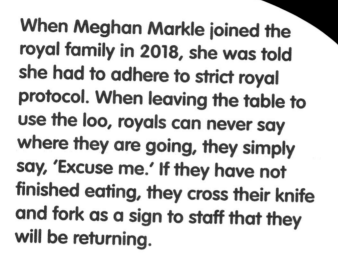

When Meghan Markle joined the royal family in 2018, she was told she had to adhere to strict royal protocol. When leaving the table to use the loo, royals can never say where they are going, they simply say, 'Excuse me.' If they have not finished eating, they cross their knife and fork as a sign to staff that they will be returning.

The cancellation of the popular Boardmasters music festival in Cornwall in 2019 left thousands of young music lovers disappointed – and a toilet supplier with 20,000 loo rolls he had to put up for sale online.

According to the charity Water Aid, what percentage of people around the world wash their hands with soap after defecating?

1. 95%
2. 19%
3. 5%
4. 62%

In one of the most memorable moments from *Lethal Weapon II*, Danny Glover is trapped sitting on a toilet which is primed to explode when he stands up.

The best position for pooing is not sitting on the toilet but squatting. Squatting puts a bend in your colon, as millions of people without toilets know to their satisfaction. In the West, it's possible to buy a squatty potty to allow you to poop in a natural position.

What's big and
brown and behind
the wall?

Humpty's Dump

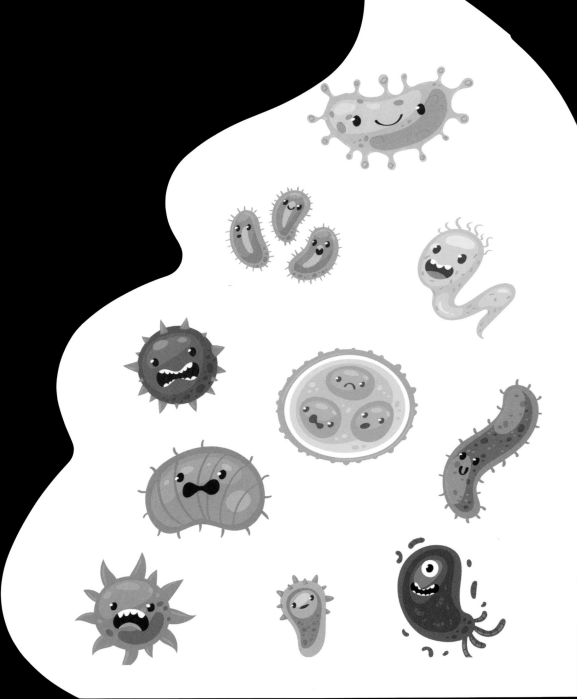

Why is poo brown?

Poo is brown because it contains dead red blood cells and bile.

Between 50 and 80 per cent of faeces – excluding water, which makes up 70 per cent of a typical poo – is bacteria that live in our intestines until they are pushed out as food passes through.

FAMOUS LOOS

A Urinal is probably the most famous loo in the history of art. It was produced by the Surrealist artist Marcel Duchamp in 1917 by taking a standard ceramic urinal and signing it 'R. Mutt.' Duchamp was one of the first artists to make readymades – pieces using existing objects.

Babies go through an average of 10,000 nappies before they are potty trained.

World Toilet Day is on 19th November. The United Nations General Assembly created it to raise awareness around the planet of the human right to clean water and sanitation.

The potty takes its name from medieval times when people used clay pots to pee in. After use, the clay pots were chucked out of the window, smashing into pieces as they hit the ground.

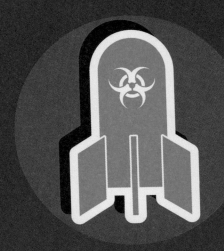

If flushing a toilet can launch
faecal bacteria into the air and
cause infections, does that make
the toilet a biological weapon?

Before the invention of toilet paper, European royalty wiped their derrière with lace.

Spot the difference between these toilet tiles

Turn to the next page for the answer.

Did you spot them?

What's the optimum number of loo paper squares needed to effectively start cleaning your bum?

a. 6

b. 3

c. 1

d. 8

Answer: b. 3. Whether you scrunch or fold is your business. Just remember to keep going until it's clean.

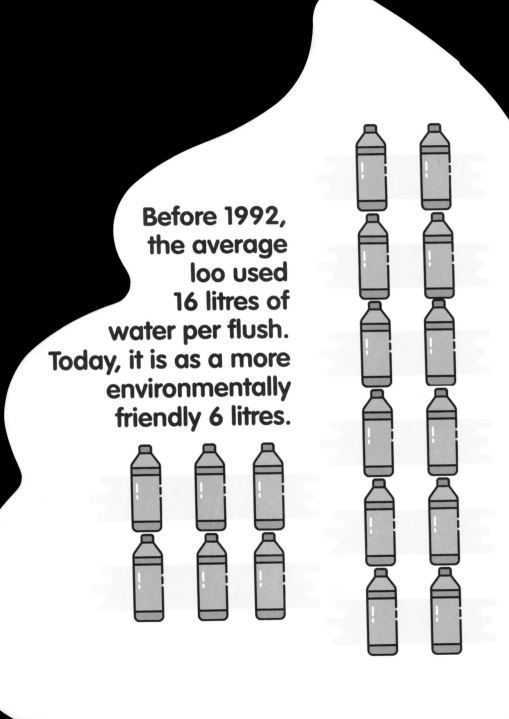

Before 1992, the average loo used 16 litres of water per flush. Today, it is as a more environmentally friendly 6 litres.

'Toilet'

comes from the French word toilette, which means 'an act of washing, dressing and preparing oneself.'

DID YOU KNOW?
Most loos flush to the key of E flat.

MOVIE MOMENT

In a scene from the hit movie *Bridesmaids*, the bride suffers with catastrophic food poisoning while being fitted for her wedding dress. She ends up pooing in the street in the dress, much to the horror of the shop's owner.

HELP THE FLY FIND ITS WAY TO THE PILE OF POO

Answer on the next page.

Did the fly make it?

A 2008 survey found that women spend on average 85 minutes and men spend 95 minutes a week on the loo.

The ancient Romans
worshipped a
goddess of sewers,
a god of the toilet
and a god of sh*t.

FAMOUS LOOS

The world's most expensive loo is in a Hong Kong gold merchant's store. The entire bathroom is finished in solid gold including the sink. The loo is made from solid gold and studded with gems. Even the tiles are made from gold. In 2010, the whole lot was valued at $29 million.

What unfortunate manner of death was shared by King Edmund II of England and Duke Godfrey IV 'The Hunchback' of Lower Lorraine?

a. They both drowned in excrement.

b. They were both stabbed in the anus.

c. They both suffered from fatal constipation.

DID YOU KNOW?

A $100,000 research project in the United States investigated the important question of whether people position their loo roll with the paper flap hanging at the front or back of the roll. Researchers discovered three out of four people had the loose paper at the front.

Urea, the main component of urine, can be used to whiten teeth. That's because it contains ammonia, which as well as being anti-bacterial, acts as a bleaching agent. The ancient Romans whitened their teeth with urine and some people still use urine today to get their gnashers sparkling!

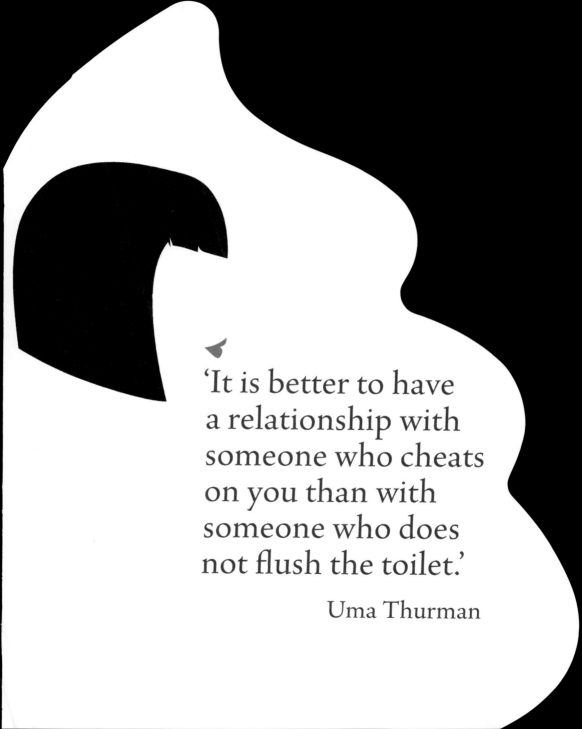

'It is better to have
a relationship with
someone who cheats
on you than with
someone who does
not flush the toilet.'

Uma Thurman

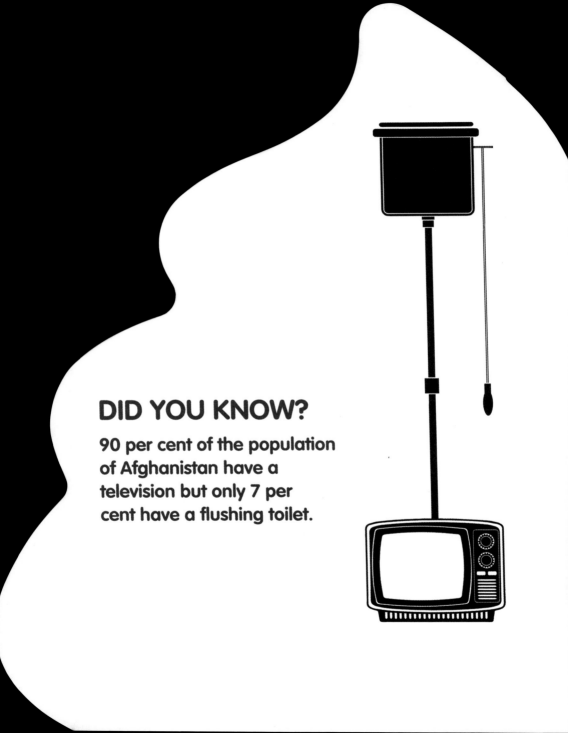

DID YOU KNOW?

90 per cent of the population of Afghanistan have a television but only 7 per cent have a flushing toilet.

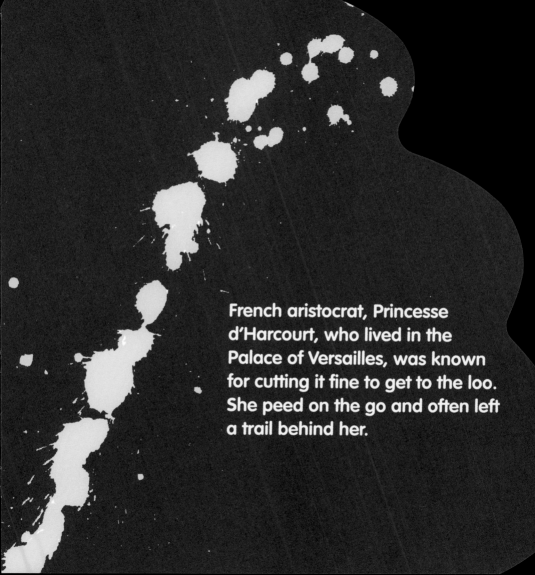

French aristocrat, Princesse d'Harcourt, who lived in the Palace of Versailles, was known for cutting it fine to get to the loo. She peed on the go and often left a trail behind her.

Did you hear about the constipated mathematician?

He worked it out with a pencil.

If you're Russian when you go into the bathroom and Finnish when you come out, what are you when you're in the bathroom?

Europeein'

DID YOU KNOW?

The Japanese always close the loo seat because germs can move as far as 2 metres out of the bowl on flushing.

Along with the Stars and Stripes and pieces of experimental equipment, the astronauts of the Moon Landing in 1969 also left on the moon four 'defecation collection devices' – NASA speak for bags of poo.

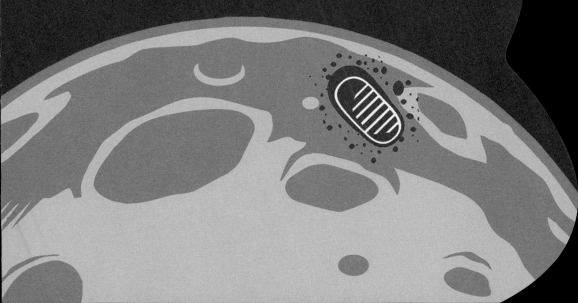

Have you seen the movie *Diarrhoea*?

It leaked so they had to release it early.

Englishman Alexander Cumming patented the world's first flushing loo in 1775. He introduced an S-bend to prevent foul smells passing back into the bowl.

In 1880, another Englishman, Thomas Crapper, improved on Cumming's invention by turning the S-bend into a U-bend.

Although Crapper is widely hailed as the inventor of the flushing toilet, he was merely a clever engineer with a gift for publicity pushing Cumming into obscurity.

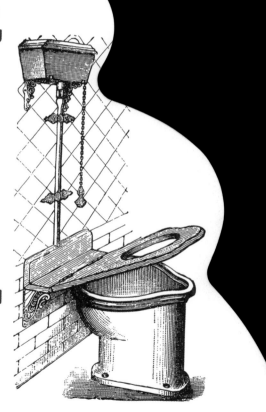

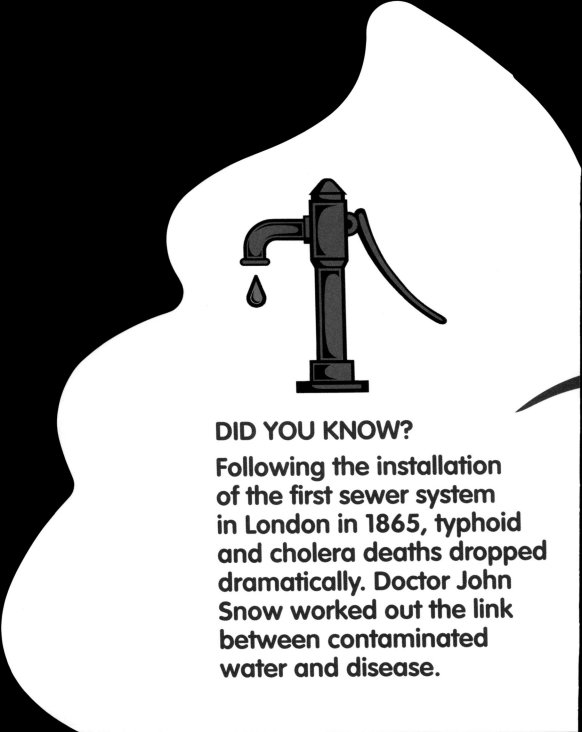

DID YOU KNOW?

Following the installation of the first sewer system in London in 1865, typhoid and cholera deaths dropped dramatically. Doctor John Snow worked out the link between contaminated water and disease.

MOVIE MOMENT

In the movie *Jurassic Park*, an unfortunate park ranger is sitting on the toilet when a T-Rex pulls down the building around him, leaving him exposed in the open air, before devouring him.

The actor who played the tiny part, Martin Ferrero, was later honoured as 'the guy who gets eaten on the toilet.'

How did King Wenceslaus III of Bohemia die in 1306?

a. Straining on the loo.

b. Speared to death on the loo.

c. He fell off the loo and hit his head.

Answer:
B. He was speared to death by a hired assassin while sitting on the loo.

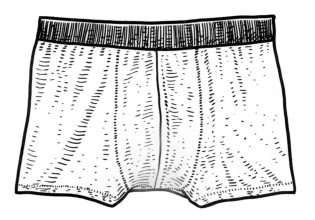

An old man takes his wife with him to the doctor's because he is hard of hearing. The doctor examines him, then says, 'We need a stool sample and a urine sample.' The man asks his wife, 'What did the doctor say?' She replies, 'He wants to see your underwear.'

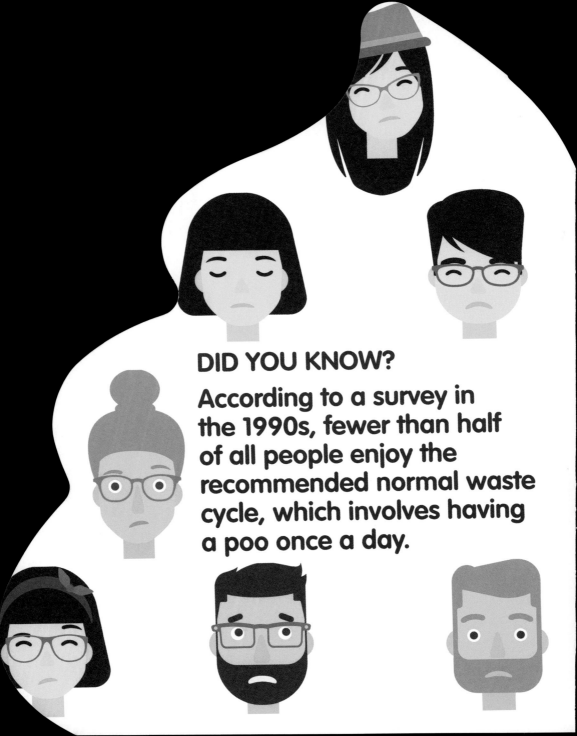

DID YOU KNOW?

According to a survey in the 1990s, fewer than half of all people enjoy the recommended normal waste cycle, which involves having a poo once a day.

The UK launched the first poo bus in 2014. It was fuelled by food waste and recycled human excrement.

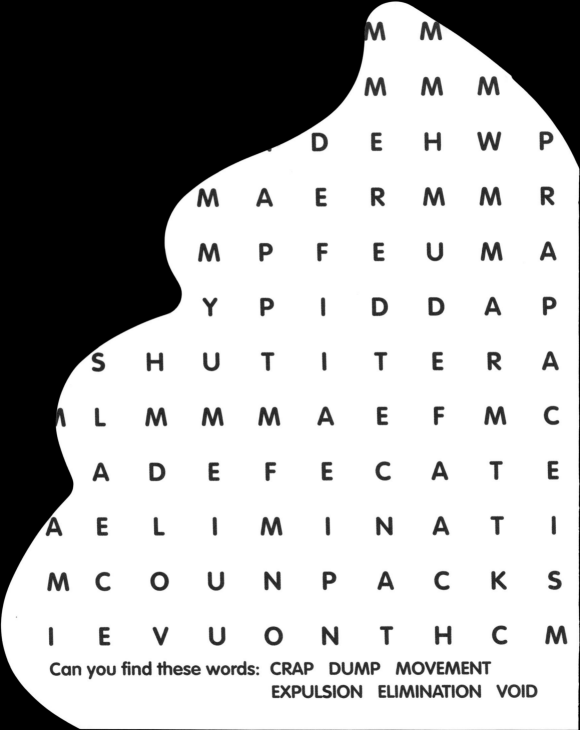

Can you find these words: CRAP DUMP MOVEMENT
EXPULSION ELIMINATION VOID

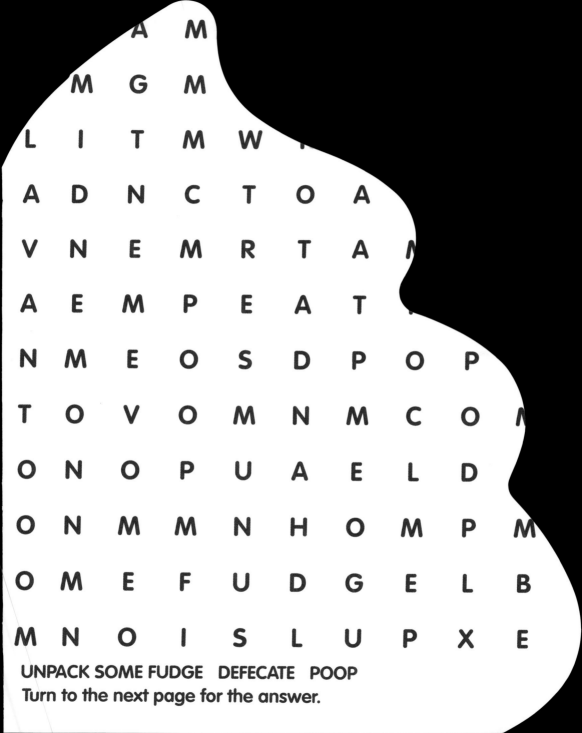

```
      A   M
   M   G   M
L  I  T  M  W  T
A  D  N  C  T  O  A
V  N  E  M  R  T  A  M
A  E  M  P  E  A  T
N  M  E  O  S  D  P  O  P
T  O  V  O  M  N  M  C  O  M
O  N  O  P  U  A  E  L  D
O  N  M  M  N  H  O  M  P  M
O  M  E  F  U  D  G  E  L  B
M  N  O  I  S  L  U  P  X  E
```

UNPACK SOME FUDGE   DEFECATE   POOP
Turn to the next page for the answer.

M M
M M M
D E H W P
M A E R M M R
M P F E U M A
Y P I D D A P
S H U T I T E R A
L M M M A E F M C
A D E F E C A T E
A E L I M I N A T I
M C O U N P A C K S
I E V U O N T H C M

```
        A   M
    M   G   M
L   I   T   M   W
A   D   N   C   T   O   A
V   N   E   M   R   T   A
A   E   M   P   E   A   T
N   M   E   O   S   D   P   O   P
T   O   V   O   M   N   M   C   O
O   N   O   P   U   A   E   L   D
O   N   M   M   N   H   O   M   P   M
O   M   E   F   U   D   G   E   L   B
M   N   O   I   S   L   U   P   X   E
```

Seen in a pub's toilet:

'Our aim is to keep this bathroom clean.

Gentlemen: Your aim will help, stand closer, it's shorter than you think.

Ladies: Please remain seated for the entire performance.'

DID YOU KNOW?

The white sand on
tropical beaches
contains around
85 per cent of poo
from the parrot fish.

What do you call
a 12-inch turd?

A foot stool

A Japanese warlord named Uesugi Kenshin was assassinated in his toilet in 1578. One of the first Ninja warriors used his training to hide in the foul pit of excrement beneath Uesugi's toilet until the warlord came to use it – when the warrior rose up and drove a spear up into his body.

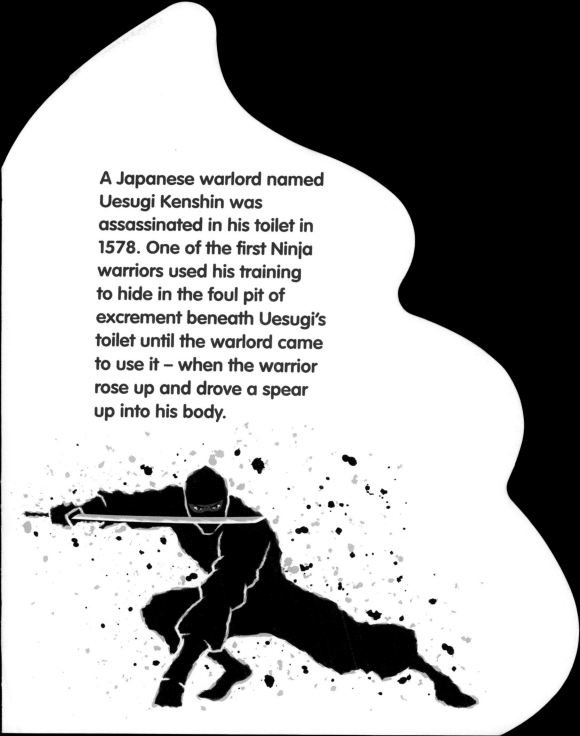

'If you lift it up, put it down again…

If you spill it, clean it up…

If it runs out, replace it…

If you're finished it, flush it…

If it smells, spray it.'

DID YOU KNOW?

Around 90 per cent of all medicine we take is excreted from our bodies through our pee. That means that water in sewerage systems in cities around the world contains a very high percentage of drugs.

Alfred Hitchcock's 1960 masterpiece *Psycho* has an unusual claim to fame. It was the first Hollywood movie to feature a loo on screen, and a flushing loo to boot! Some outraged movie-goers accused the film and Hitchcock of promoting indecency.

FAMOUS LOOS

The world's most high-tech and expensive loo is the Japanese Toto, which includes jets of water to wash your bum and a dryer for afterwards; a heated seat for those chilly mornings; automatic de-deodorisation and a function known as the 'marriage saver' that automatically puts the seat down after use.

MOVIE MOMENT

In the classic gangster movie, *The Godfather*, Michael Corleone, played by Al Pacino, is the straight man of the family until he assassinates two rivals in a restaurant using a gun that has been hidden in classic movie style behind – the toilet cistern.

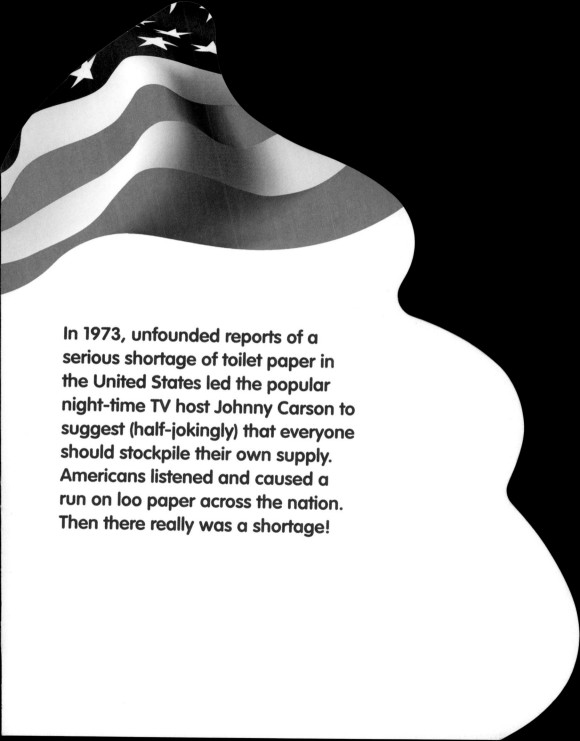

In 1973, unfounded reports of a serious shortage of toilet paper in the United States led the popular night-time TV host Johnny Carson to suggest (half-jokingly) that everyone should stockpile their own supply. Americans listened and caused a run on loo paper across the nation. Then there really was a shortage!

DID YOU KNOW?

Some 78 per cent of UK couples say that bathroom habits – who left the loo seat up? – are a bigger cause of arguments than money.

Did you know that diarrhoea is hereditary?

It runs in your genes.

WE VANDALISE
THINGS THAT
AREN'T OURS

WITH QUOTES
WE DIDN'T WRITE

TO IMPRESS PEOPLE
TAKING SH*TS.

DID YOU KNOW?

Around 42 million Americans suffer from constipation. Laxatives are big business – worth around $1.38 billion in 2018.

The lock with a vacant/engaged sign on a public loo was patented by a British inventor named Mr Ashwell in South London in 1883.

For the ancient
Egyptians, the loo was
called 'the House of
Morning.'

For the ancient Israelites,
it was the 'House of
Honour.'

Barbara is sailing by ship from the south of the equator to the north. She has a lovely interior cabin with its own bathroom but no window. How can she tell when the ship crosses the equator?

Answer:

If she fills the sink then watches the water drain, it will change from draining in an anticlockwise direction south of the equator to a clockwise direction in the Northern Hemisphere.

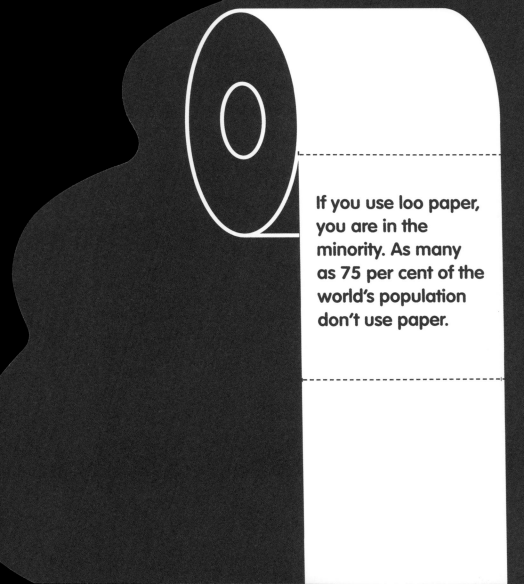

If you use loo paper, you are in the minority. As many as 75 per cent of the world's population don't use paper.

DID YOU KNOW?

According to WHO,
2 billion people
around the world
do not have basic
sanitation. Of them,
673 million still
go in the open –
in gutters, rivers,
or behind bushes.

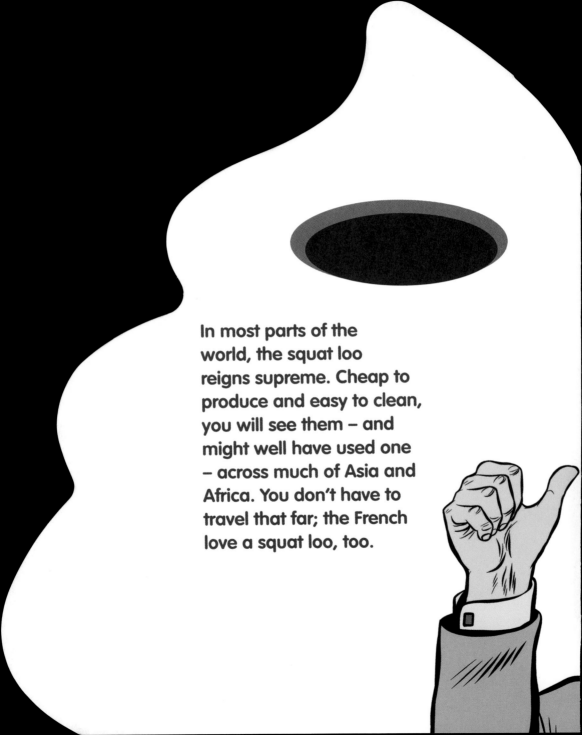

In most parts of the world, the squat loo reigns supreme. Cheap to produce and easy to clean, you will see them – and might well have used one – across much of Asia and Africa. You don't have to travel that far; the French love a squat loo, too.

Urine was used in World War I in gas masks. Scientists, wrongly it was later found out, thought that the ammonia in urine would neutralize the chlorine in chlorine gas. In fact, the opposite was true. The ammonia reacted with the chlorine to produce toxic fumes.

History has long told us that King George III of Britain, who ruled between 1760 and 1814, suffered from porphyria which sent him mad. One of the symptoms of porphyria is purple pee, but his was blue. Recent research suggests it was, in fact, his medicine that turned his pee blue. It contained the plant gentian. Gentian's deep blue flowers can turn pee blue. Watch out, as it's still used as a mild tonic.

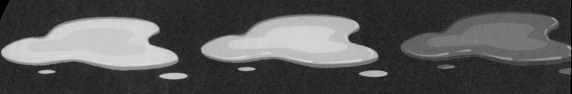

DID YOU KNOW?

The average porcelain loo lasts 50 years.

A British divorce lawyer once had to fight on her client's behalf for a toilet seat. The object of the struggle had been a wedding present, and both husband and wife claimed that it had emotional value for them.

What do you call Clark Kent with diarrhoea?

Pooperman

HERE I SIT, BROKEN HEARTED.

CAME TO SH*T BUT ONLY FARTED.

'Things I hate:
  1. Vandalism
  2. Lists
  3. Irony
  4. Lists
  5. Repetition
  F. Inconsistency.'

DID YOU KNOW?

To kill bacteria effectively after using the loo, you need to wash your hands with soap for a minimum of 20 seconds. Only 5 per cent of all people do so.

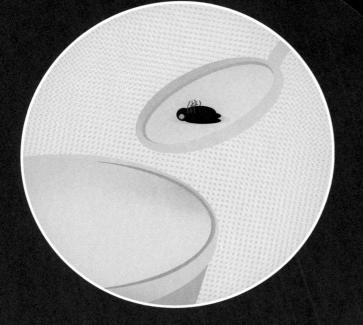

'Waiter, what's this fly
doing in my soup?'

'Pooping.'

'It's not hard to tell we was poor – when you saw the toilet paper dryin' on the clothesline.'

George Lindsey

In many of the world's cultures where people eat using their right hand, it is considered taboo to use the left hand for anything except wiping your bum post-loo.

It was only in the 19th century that seated loos entered the mass market. Today, they are used almost exclusively in western and northern Europe, Australia, New Zealand and the United States.

What's brown and firm?

The Brown Family Law Firm

Urine therapy – drinking your own pee – is popular in Germany where nearly 5 million people drink their own pee regularly. These people believe their pee is a health tonic, but there is no scientific evidence to back that up.

In medieval European castles there was a separate room for the loo. The garderobe came with a special hole in the floor so all the crap and pee fell directly into a cesspit or moat. An added bonus was that clothes and precious items were stored in the room because it was believed ammonia from the pee killed moths and fleas.

Doctors in ancient Greece believed that donkey pee could cure insanity.

One in five adults has admitted to peeing in a public swimming pool. The red eyes you suffer isn't a reaction to the pool's chlorine. It's a reaction to the chemicals produced by the pee mixing with the chlorine.

Yikes!

What do you call a
vegetarian with diarrhoea?

A Salad Shooter

DID YOU KNOW?

More than 70 per cent of shopping trolleys in U.S. supermarkets tested positive for traces of human excrement on the handles.

'You must know that it is by the state of the lavatory that a family is judged.'

Pope John XXIII

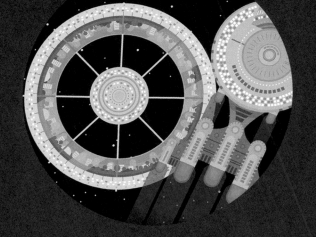

What do loo paper and
the Starship *Enterprise*
have in common?

They both fly around
Uranus looking for
Klingons.

IF YOU
SPRINKLE
WHEN YOU
TINKLE,

PLEASE BE
SWEET

AND WIPE
THE SEAT.

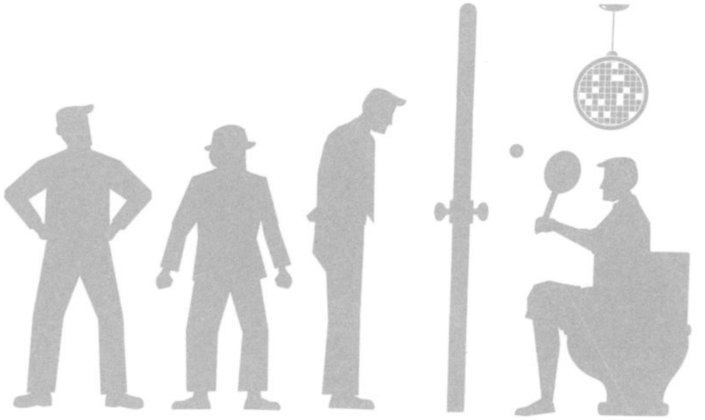